HAUNTED MARSHALL

BRIAN MASON

Wynwidyn PRESS

Pinckney, Mi

ISBN: 978-1-941737-20-0
Published by Wynwidyn Press, LLC
~In conjunction with
E. B. Finbryton & Associates.

Cover Photography courtesy of Brian Hawkins.
Cover Design: Cara Maib (www.cara-maib-design.com)
Layout Design: Bob Houston eBook Formatting
For additional information: www.hauntedmarshall.com

Haunted Marshall

Ghosts, legends and folklore in Michigan's most paranormal town

"There are no truths, only stories"
Thomas King

For my wife Courtney, my boys and beautiful daughter: Your love is enough and I am truly amazed at your sacrifices during the years of chasing this dream.

I am home now and there will never be another lost day.

To all the dreamers who went along with me at different points on this adventure: it was my esteemed pleasure to have met all of you.

This book is for everyone, even the ones who didn't believe....

AGTSP

Introduction

In the beginning

As the winds of life would have it, I, without notice, blew into a somewhat lost and forgotten city named Marshall, MI in the year of 2008. It is a charming place of grand Victorian homes, some of which seem to touch the sky, and there is a subtle hint of polite secrecy amongst its inhabitants, especially those fondly known as "Marshallites." Charming and full of enchantment, it has a quaint downtown that is mixed with neat little shops, restaurants and even a two-screened family-owned movie theatre that gives away free popcorn on Monday nights if you bring your own bowl. The streets bustle with people, even into the late hours, as neighbors and guests stroll through town, most of whom are on their way, especially during the summer months, to the Brooks Memorial Fountain, a focal point of town. It is a grand replica of Marie Antionette's fountain "Temple of Love" in Versailles, France and has been adorning the town since 1930. It stands greeting guests who enter the city with its splashing water and an evening light show. I think one would be hard pressed to find another place with such fond visual appeal that also has an air to it that is vaguely familiar and welcoming, yet a bit oddly quiet and mysterious.

I found myself entranced and captivated by its beauty and mystery from my first visit. I knew that many of these structures had stories to tell. I remember one of my first nightly walks when I so vividly found that there seemed as if a voice that spoke to me from the trees, the homes and the buildings. I thought I was going crazy but as my strolls continued night after night I knew I was not alone and that there was something reaching out to me, something I was to encounter myself. So, with the time and circumstances of the universe, I began what has now been a nine-year journey into my legacy of the beyond, something that has become...my haunted Marshall.

From the viewpoint of a little farm that lays on the east side of the city along Michigan Avenue, I have a take unlike any other of a quaint, obscure town where history is alive, for me, through death. As I gaze out my window at the snow-covered field where our horses are at a much-needed winter break and the wind is wisping the flakes across the frozen ground, I reflect on my collection of tales given to me as a gift to share. The carriages and wagons are tucked away with a few leftover Halloween decorations flowing in the breeze of this cold January day. The cars roll pass as some of them stop at our favorite little red party store, *Warmans*, that is neighboring the farm. The kids have nicknamed it "the little store that lives next door." It is the local beer and lottery stop with killer food and a local favorite where the kids stroll the isles for many sweet treasures abound. This is the day that I have decided to tell my story. A story in which my family has made a business of touring the paranormal of Marshall, Mi. It has become a daily activity to us and I don't even have much of a memory of how or why it all happened…I just know that it did and it is time to share it with you before it is lost again.

The kitchen table is scattered with books and papers as I make my way into my own mind to fashion what I consider one of the best cases for hauntings I have ever encountered: Marshall Michigan. I have traveled and made home to many towns but have rarely known any with such passion. I have lived in this delightful place for almost nine years at this point, guided here by God only knows what divine force. I stretched myself as far as I could for the embrace of these stories through personal challenges, homelessness and political strife. These pages are made with blood and sweat and love. They are everything that I had to give, everything I strived to create.

My wife is curled up on the couch studying diligently for Medical School as I pound away on this keyboard, delving into the paranormal that haunts my brain, each of us with our own dream. Luckily, she has taken many breaks to help revive some of what I have forgotten in our journey. Her attention to detail is invaluable and her memory of my journey, especially at the end remind me of where I am headed and why this book had to be written.

We have roamed these streets in search of what makes this one of the most haunted towns one may ever encounter. Though the minutes have turned into days and soon to years, I have watched as the stories that are here within awakened from deep inside the people that told them, forever a part of them now. Forever a part of their legends and a part of their community, even after I am gone. Whether they are fact or imagined or likely a combination of both, I have somehow been able to reach deep within the subconscious of this little city and pull out a part of it that we all have locked away, hidden inside. It is the innate notion that there must be something else and that each of us has our own story to tell that is lingering just at the tip of our tongues. It is the underlying hope that none of this really ends and somehow, we too shall become immortal in death.

Marshall, Michigan, the almost town, or little town that couldn't, rests in the heart of the state. It was founded in

1839 ish, depending on what sign you read and has had a vast history of successes and failures, including losing the vote for State Capitol. From the gun-slinging saloon days to the cocaine rush, some claim Marshall is defined by her houses but I maintain she is defined by the lingering secrets that roam those pale dusty hallowed halls who have awaited their story told, who awaited my arrival.

I have claimed Marshall to be the most haunted town in Michigan and that lies mainly on the fact that in all my travels I have yet to encounter a town with such a vast collection of paranormal experiences that have either been passed down or made up, perhaps even by me. It is, in part, a game of telephone, but deeply rooted in every story is the spark from which it had its inception, a truth. It is said that there are no truths but only stories and perhaps that fact remains, yet it is in the story that we find the imagination of the very people by whom they were constructed.

Bringing people together for a good tale has always been a delight of mine. It is in my nature to find magic in the most obscure places but, in Marshall, the stories just came to me one after another almost effortlessly. After these years of gathering and telling these stories countless times, I decided it was time to immortalize them for the next generations and for those who have not had the chance as I did to relish in the sheer mystery and the lives of the people they have touched. I was sent out on a mission from somewhere and happened upon here and the time to share is now. I believe this book will allow others from near and far to find a place where the unexplainable exists in rare and true form, and invite the readers to come for themselves to experience the mystery of Marshall.

It is a place wherein the dreams of the dearly departed continue to manifest even from beyond and once this is written, my work is done. The lurking tales of Marshall can now be experienced and shared over and over again throughout time immemorial. It is a survival plan of sorts. It is my way of leaving something as an appreciation for the time. It is my insurance that the tales won't disappear and are not eternally lost. Through these pages they will all live just as they have been spoken to me. All my friends will have mortality through print.

I and many others have called Marshall the "almost town" or the "little town that couldn't", mostly in jest, and that is because of the many, if not peculiar, ups and downs it has experienced since its inception in 1830 by Sidney Ketchum. For many of the residents throughout history, there were dreams that were never realized for one reason of another. First, Marshall was to be the state capitol, which legend says it lost by only one vote. Then there was the railroad which blazed through and promised for a new prosperity, which eventually relocated to Jackson much to the disappointment and economic downfall of many. The challenges continued as the patent medicine days began and the city was well on its way to being the capitol of that industry until the inception of the FDA in 1906, which forced its demise. The snake oil business dried up and Marshall faltered.

For decades people have been flocking here with the next best idea to move Marshall into success, mostly to no avail, but to outsiders, success is already here. Therein this city is a living breathing masterpiece of mostly untouched history. It has survived all the turmoil and tests of time still standing much as it always has, preserved by its shortcomings. That is its triumph and its measured success is invaluable in comparison. While many little towns withered away, Marshall has remained with a vibrant community of believers still awaiting their reckoning. Even the evil empires that have tried to tear her apart and separate her people have been subdued by the relentless passion of those within her care. There is an air of longing here always on the horizon. There is a vision that continues to be protected.

It is that very passion that renders Marshall's undead restless. The paranormal lurk around every corner and know no bounds, from the city streets and glorious mansions to the humble worker homes and downtown shops. Even our cemeteries host a variety of haunts, legend and lore. The city that has been known for many things throughout history is perhaps less known, until now, for their "other" side. The paranormal appears to have been alive and well much before my time but perhaps only talked about around burning fall fires or over pints with the odd lucky traveler, but still mostly a secret.

I encountered my first real haunting in the first home I purchased here. It was months after experiencing countless odd happenings of my own that I began to venture out; asking more questions, longing for more knowledge. In doing so I found much more than I anticipated. I had always felt something here amongst these old pieces of history but what I was privy to existed far deeper within the community than I had anticipated. Some eager residents were all too willing to tell their story. Most of whom likely had no idea that it would draw so much attention.

From my first visit to town I had been struck with the idea of bringing horses here to reinvent part of a lost historic element of the community. It is something that I felt would fit and so early in 2009 I stopped by this little farm on the east end of Michigan Ave. and met the owner. I asked if he might be interested in leasing his barn and property. It was a perfect location of about four acres just outside of the city limits with a convenient street that led to town without traffic. Initially, I was met with a resounding "no!" and it wasn't until several minutes into the conversation that I had the opportunity to explain my purpose for wanting to rent and the opportunity to present my ideas for the community. Shortly thereafter I was making a deal to seal the new dream. I ordered my first horse and carriage from Florida and awaited its arrival while I pondered with city council the next steps.

Marshall was eager to help, to have this plan realized and, while I had no idea what I was doing, struck up a deal to rent a spot in a building that the city owned at a fair price to get me started. Parking was granted on Michigan Ave. for the horses and we were well on our way.

I began hosting historical tours of this beautiful city in the spring of 2010 with the inception of Marshall Carriage Co., a modest horse drawn business. We quickly added 'Ghost Tours' to its repertoire and its name after the influx of paranormal stories I had started collecting. I hired a few local believers to join me on this journey and opened in July of that year. Within a few weeks we had a line of eager passengers, acquired another horse and carriage and were well on the way to realizing the dream. Residents showed up and offered a hand at the stables or in town. Horse lovers came with knowledge and pointers and the whole plan moved along without a hitch. Today, the company boasts enough vehicles to move more than a few dozen passenger per tour, owns the world's only horse drawn ice cream business and has expanded into walking and dinner tours, all while seeing thousands of visitors per year. It quickly became the face of the city and we loved every minute of it.

As all good stories go there have been ups and downs along with business and personal strife, yet our family maintained a steady operation for seven years, eventually selling in 2016, moving on to other ambitions, mainly myself as an author and my wife to medical school at MSU College of Osteopathic Medicine. I believe whole heartedly that it is by the grace of Marshall's energy that we had been allowed to continue, weathering what challenges may have come. I also believe I was sent here on a mission or lured here by a force that wanted and needed to have its story told. The carriage company was only the vehicle for me to maneuver through. I have always listened to the breezes of my life and this time it called me to Marshall. It was by pure accident that I ended up here and by pure magic that the community was eager to share their deepest, darkest and most treasured stories. The city of Marshall holds more than just ghost stories and we have only scratched the surface of the depth of its mystery. This is the story of the paranormal, that which goes bump in the night, all that is left of the dreams and ambitions of those who have gone before, and I have attempted to tell it in the best fashion I can just as it was gently and cautiously shared with me.

Being haunted is not just about ghosts; it is about the unraveling of stories that have been left untold through ages of deceit and passion. It is about happenings that have not yet been rectified, or perhaps, shuffled away and left only in the memories of those who wish to hide their secrets. Some stories are lost forever to death who stands eternally zip lipped. Marshall has those secrets and I have made it my mission to find answers for both those who wish to hear and for those whose voices have been muffled throughout time.

As the shadows of evening fall, I am left at this keyboard, my light dimly lit, to begin my tales, each with its own invigorating plot. I invite you to travel along with me through these pages, to be a part of Michigan's most haunted town ... one of America's most paranormal places. Indeed, it goes without saying that there are legends near and far in all corners of the world, but after all these years of study, within are compiled a comprehensive list that rivals most others. It is a collection of stories that deserve attention and have their eternal place amongst local lore. I hope you fondly relish these fables for what they are worth and I implore you to visit Marshall, MI to witness firsthand what has been the best kept paranormal secret ever brought forth. One day, this city will see its fruition, of a place where history is alive through death and then those who have lingered beyond their graves, who have whispered to my ears their stories, will finally be resolved and free. Of this I am certain. This whole story is of a man, a horse and a dream that was bigger than himself, that consumed him for a large span of his life, no matter the cost. This is my version…

Hauntingly yours,

Brian Mason

Clinton T. Cook House

Owned currently by the Harnden family, this 1886 Queen Anne Victorian home was once the build of Clinton T. Cook, one of Marshall's first grocers. Built entirely out of brick, which was quite a monetary feat of the day, leaves this home as one of the most expensive of its time. Mr. Cook's grocery store was located where the Bogar Theatre stands today and many pictures adorn the wall depicting that history. It isn't clear how long Clinton lived in this property prior to his death, but it is clear that it was constructed as an heir to his family later in his life, which was a common practice.

In 2003, the Harndens purchased the home and moved here from St. Louis after falling in love with Marshall several years prior. That story, in and of itself, is of a magical setting as the couple fell into the purchase almost divinely. They were meant to have it. That being said, the Harndens were in for a terrific and spiritual encounter that would begin upon their arrival to Marshall and continue to this day.

I had the esteemed pleasure of meeting the couple shortly upon my moving to Marshall in 2009 and, after purchasing my own haunted home, was quickly introduced along with a host of other families who had experienced paranormal on a regular basis. It had quickly come to my attention that Marshall hosted a great number of tales and legends that extended beyond my own experiences which lead me to begin to investigate these stories in depth.

The following is the accounts of the Harnden Family:

Scott and Holly Harnden longed for a town just like Marshall, Michigan and had traveled here many years adoring the architecture and charm of a small mid-western city unlike many they had ever encountered. After countless visits, they had the chance they had always dreamed of to purchase a historic home on the corner of Mansion and High St. It was surreal and the couple made the decision to make the move and find their future there.

The very first inclination of something odd happened directly at the closing when the previous owners asked to speak with the couple about a story they wished to pass down about their own experiences in the home. They explained that many years earlier, they purchased a toy cash register which much to their surprise had taken on a life of its own. It would ring and make noises, even having the cash drawer open, all on its own accord. Shocked at this paranormal event, the family quickly gave credit to the home's builder Clinton T. Cook, as they felt perhaps he found amusement in playing with this item in the after-life that he most certainly used often in life years prior. The Harndens were told that the previous owners had left the little toy on the kitchen counter as they felt Mr. Cook would want it to stay. The home passed to the new owners and they began to move in. All the while the toy cash register sat in its place on the kitchen counter.

The couple had told us that it wasn't until the second weekend that they were at the home bringing in their belongings that they had their first encounter. They were taking a break from moving and decided to sit in the dining room and have lunch when they began to hear a beeping noise. Within a few seconds they heard a ding and the sound of a drawer opening, just like a cash register. In disbelief, they looked at each other and immediately made their way to the adjoining kitchen to investigate finding the drawer to be open. From that point on they heard noises quite often in resemblance to the ding and beeps likened to that toy. It eventually made its way into the basement but could still be heard in a muffled sound from time to time so the Harndens placed it in a bin in the attic where is still is today and can be heard on occasion -- depending on where you are in the home.

Many other happenings that cannot be explained have also inhibited the lives of this family including steps being heard, doors creaking open and shut and a host of eerie sounds. Mr. Cook has made himself right at home with the Harnden family and they have welcomed him in as part of their family and part of the home they fell in love with. He has even been known to turn on the shower while Mrs. Harnden is cleaning the tub and has on occasion filled the tub himself only for the family to find it almost overflowing just in the nick of time.

Probably the most entertaining story, one that could show how much a spirit can be attached to something they hold dear beyond death, happened at this home in January of 2013. Mr. Harnden decided to take a nap in his recliner while his wife was out enjoying town on Saturday afternoon. Much to his amazement he was jolted awake by the recliner tipping back in a fast motion. He awoke calling the name of his wife but she was nowhere to be found. Figuring he had just had a dream of sorts he decided to rest his eyes again. The explanation to us is that he then fell asleep and was awoken again with about four to five violent rocking motions, this time jumping to his feet, rolling out of the chair. Nothing again! Moments later he sniffed the air and smelled smoke. Immediately, he left the room to find the location from which this smell was coming from. After quickly moving through the house, he became aware that the couple's bedroom was on fire due to an old electric blanket being left on.

Mr. Harnden was able to put the fire out with extinguishers and diligently continued his way in more than once to save the home of their dreams. All the while, sirens could be heard making their way down the city streets to the home. He headed in for one last spray after he convinced the firemen to let him finish putting out the flames to avoid any further damage to the house. The fire was all but out by this time.

I remember having one of the staff members of the city fire department on tour with us. He explained how Mr. Harnden had awakened to find the fire a blaze. The home was severely damaged by smoke and the family even lost pets, but this fire could have been so much worse had whatever awakened Mr. Harnden not have happened. The family, to this day, still tells the story of how their ghost, whom they call Clinton T. Cook, saved the home they share a deep love with.

This was one of the very first homes that caught my eye and certainly one of the first stories I heard concerning Marshall's paranormal. Not only is this a gem of a home, it is also a fantastic example of how people in this little town have coexisted with the afterlife. We have visited this home on our ghost tour countless nights, witnessing everything from orbs to visits from the Harndens themselves as they keep us current on new haunts. This home is a fantastic piece of history and is a gem of this great town. The family and their friendship helped to mold my experiences with the paranormal in Marshall and to them, I am forever indebted.

Mrs. Harnden was kind enough to lead me to our next story and so my journey continued, inspired by her passion for Marshall...

The Pace Mansion and the Occult

The Gibbs-Lacey house was built in 1838 atop the highest point in Marshall at 326 High St. Over the years it has been affectionately known as the Pace mansion, as their family owned the home the longest of all its inhabitants. Don Pace was the last of its owners, passing away some years ago at the age of 107. It is said that he walked to town up until 105. He was a stern man and held a secret that was shared and experienced by only one lucky fellow who happened to find Marshall in much the same way I did. Chance.

Near retirement age, Emerson Shelby, whom I have had the distinct pleasure of knowing well, moved to Marshall to care for an aging Don Pace. Emerson had been in theatre and radio in New York City for many years although he was a native of Flint, Michigan. His dear friend, Hunter Ligget, was a nephew to Mr. Pace and had received word that his uncle, needed a temporary caretaker because he had broken a hip and only needed a month or so of care, or so they had assumed. Hunter opted to leave New York and come to take on the task, asking Emerson to tag along and then the two could take a much-needed rest in the quaint little town of Marshall. Emerson was up for the journey at hand and the two friends ventured out on what would change one of them forever.

The two men made their way from New York to a new city that had been trapped in time, concluding their journey at the dark, eerie mansion that stood deep in a midst of overhanging trees. It was said that the Pace family had owned the property for over a hundred years and that Don Pace was the last of the empire. Fairly early on it was learned that poor Don would need someone to continue care much longer than originally thought and Emerson decided, knowing that he was near retirement, to take on the task.

Mr. Pace gave him an apartment to live in that was attached to the North side of the mansion. The two made an agreement and Emerson was told that he must be made aware of the supernatural events that inhibited the home. Don explained to him that the home was not only haunted but that it was "jumping" with spirits from the beyond.

Mr. Pace shared with him that their family had been a part of the occult for many years and that people used to come to the mansion eager to contact the dead with the help of the various members of his family. He was adamant in the fact that souls had been trapped between the world of the living and the dead, lingering around every corner of the mansion with unrest for various reasons. Stranger still, none of these souls had ever actually lived there, but were, rather, stuck.

I had the opportunity to sit with Emerson on many occasions discussing the events at 326 High St. and am confident that, although somewhat diluted over time, the stories must have some basis in reality. He had become a regular both at my business downtown and at my kitchen table as we rolled the days and nights away with stories of his life, my business and the mysterious Pace residence. Emerson was certainly a teller of tales, but there was a bit of ambiguity to him and I felt as if he knew something more than what he ever said. He was elusive, but intelligent beyond words, a true poet and thinker.

Mr. Pace had confided in Emerson on numerous occasions concerning that which kept him up in the night and why. Mostly filled with souls that were contacted through seances and such as people pressed forward to use the Pace family for some sort of comfort regarding their dead. Don had even showed Emerson where a 'supposed' portal or pathway existed by the back Southwestern portion of the property. It allowed the deceased to travel between our dimension and theirs. It is a fascinating story and one that Mr. Shelby believed whole heartedly and still does. There was even a Swedish gardener who worked for the Pace family and was said to have disappeared on that part of the property, leaving only a hat and a rake behind. Some say he can be seen some days looking over the South side of the property facing Oaklawn Hospital and was reported to appear more often after houses were removed for hospital expansion. It seemed farfetched, but the story has never wavered.

As Emerson and I dove head first into the occult dealings of the Pace mansion, I soon realized that he was an intricate part of the story as he had experienced most of the legends surrounding this home himself: from the elderly lady in white that walked up and down the staircase to the poltergeist that tugged at clothing and bed sheets in the middle of the night.

He was and is the only vessel left to keep the Pace stories of the dead alive! He was the last person who was close with Don and I spent countless days listening to his tales. It was Don who kept the home and stayed as its occupant to save others from experiencing that which they would not understand as he did. It was his fate and his job, as he told Emerson, to keep the spirits safe from those who didn't or wouldn't take care of them.

The home was built at a time when the Potawatomi were still prevalent and lived not far up the road. They roamed past the Pace mansion daily on their way to the rivers to trade or travel. They are but a casino away now and the trace of them within Marshall is all but dust. That in itself is a mystery and probably best kept for another conversation! The mansion had shutters adorning the windows on both the outside and the inside; the outside ones for the weather and the inside ones for privacy from native passersby. The home is a Gothic Revival that has been owned by two separate parities since I have resided in Marshall and I have had the privilege of speaking with both the families concerning the paranormal!

There was also a benevolent poltergeist that happened to mostly inhabit the kitchen and loved to make sure the cabinets stayed open when active. This was confirmed by Emerson and the subsequent owner, Mr. R., as well. One such story existed where the cupboards were even held shut by rubber bands only to have been opened during the night with all of the bands piled neatly on the counter the next morning.

The first and foremost accounts come from Emerson Shelby, who brought the story to me and by whom I was most graciously introduced to by Mrs. Harnden of the Cook house. Emerson is a delightful chap of seventyish and who boasts an eccentric nature full of mystery and intrigue. He has a rich background in the arts and claims Marshall his last stop. Souls like Emerson only come into your life but maybe once. I can say he lead me on this journey of tales from the part of Marshall's history that is unknown to most of its visitors. We have spoken for countless hours and he has regaled me with tales of the Pace mansion and the happenings he has experienced throughout his years living on the property, both with Mr. Pace and subsequent owners after. He was the second to inspire me to continue my quest for answers.

The Curse of Abner Pratt

Abner Pratt was born in 1801 and died in 1863. He was a brassy man with a loud voice and a head of wild hair. He also was one of Marshall's Mayors and a leader whose fame is in the history books forever, He was also one who had a secret that was tarnished and tattered leaving a trail of misfortune and misery until his last breath. Yet still, to this day, for some strange reason is rarely talked about. His sixty-two years, to me, are all cumulated in one story of horrific misconduct towards his fellow humanity, the least part of which is the money he took.

Before Pratt's death, he constructed in Marshall what would become a center point of architecture: the famed Honolulu House. The home is of Polynesian style and is now a museum owned by the Marshall Historical Society. It holds resemblance to the Hawaiian palace of Kamehameha IV and Queen Emma which no longer exists. The museum is open to visitors and includes a full tour with a few of the "minor" details left out, perhaps for prosperity. I found myself digging a little deeper into how a man who made such modest money could afford to construct such an expansive and expensive home.

It appeared that he had "dumped" a large sum of money before he passed. I also noticed that the gravestones of both Pratt and his wife were extremely small and not at all indicative of the money they were said to have had. It appeared to me that they were either wealthy philanthropists or broke. I also noticed that they were buried at the foot of one Charles Gorham, who was the town banker during this time and an extremely wealthy man. Gorham had his own set of stories, but I shall save these for another time.

Abner Pratt was indeed a well-off man during his working years and he had made most of his money (likely illegally) while serving as the consulate of the Hawaiian

Islands, appointed by President James Buchan 1857. He served until 1859 when, as the story goes, he returned to his much-loved Marshall, MI and constructed his home inspired by the islands he so loved.

What most fail to mention, as they tell a veiled romantic story is that Abner had accumulated a sum of blood money and left a trail of deceit and destruction including the possible death of 150 people from his days in Hawaii. He dumped most of it in Marshall, MI, keeping its origins hidden. Pratt had constructed a few other homes in town, including the one across the street (currently Chemical Bank). That one was for his daughter and son-in-law and the tale has been passed down that he built it that close so he could keep an eye on them. The Honolulu house is said to have  been the most expensive home built in Marshall, likely even by today's standards, at a whopping $20,000.

In today's standards, that would be estimated around $520,000, thus likely still one of the most expensive homes. Abner earned roughly $4,000 per year as a consulate, not including monies he took above and beyond from poor unsuspecting individuals.

In 1863 Pratt was in the Michigan House of Representatives and commuted from Marshall to Lansing. As the story goes, he rode his horse dressed in Hawaiian linens, and contracted pneumonia during in the inclement Michigan weather and died. It isn't even known if he ever resided in the Honolulu house as it is thought that he took up residence in his daughter's home due to declining health. Upon his death, however, his financial ruin and deception caught up with him (another part of Marshall's forgotten history) as the mansion was seized and sold at debtor's auction for approximately $4,000. Mr. Pratt died penniless and my suspicions began to be realized upon hearing this story.

Because of his position as Consulate in the Hawaiian Islands, Abner Pratt, found himself in a convenient position to misappropriate funds allowed him by the government and to also misuse his power to commit people to a slavery of sorts aiding his financial benefit. The United States granted money to care for sailors who came to port, including medical, clothing and food, and would pay for medical care, however, it was believed that Mr. Pratt misallocated those funds into his own pocket and likely even the pocket of the Purveyor of the hospital in Honolulu and one Dr. Guillou.

Seamen were retained in the hospital well after their needed time, sent to town to work, only to report back to the hospital nightly siting that they still needed medical care. Essentially, they were held hostage and never medically released yet used for the profit of the men in control. They were forced to sign blank receipts and then those receipts were filled in with exorbitant expenses and sent to Washington for reimbursement.

A man named Robert Left, a shoemaker in Honolulu and a victim of this scandalous scheme for nine long months, testified, along with others, that this sort of act had gone on for years. He claimed that many men were well and could have been discharged, but were trapped in this evil tale of human slavery. It is known that many people were involved or, at the very least, had knowledge of these misdoings, including the Captains of the ships. It is estimated that a sum of at least $9,000 per year was possibly improperly allocated, but no one is sure of the actual number. Basically, Abner Pratt was a thief and a con-artist, who spent the later years of his life imprisoning people for profit and returned to Marshall likely to hide and escape his wrongdoings. His sins would soon follow, but it would be too late for vindication.

Later in 1860, six months after Pratt left the islands, a ship named the *USS Levant* rolled into port carrying Commander William Hunt. He, along with the top representative for the State Department in Hawaii, US Commissioner James W. Borden, investigated the claims against Pratt. Two versions of the story came to light, one by each man, however; the version by Hunt was the one sent back to Washington via the *Levant*. It never made it.

The *USS Levant*, 150 crew and the report vanished, never to be seen again. It was thought to be a typhoon that sunk the ship. Yet wasn't it ironic that Hunt had made two copies of the report? The second copy was given to a newspaper reporter who was instructed to publish it in the event that anything should "happen" to the *Levant*. Imagine the irony.

Borden's version of the events did, however, make it to Washington. Abner Pratt was caught at last. Unfortunately, by the time the authorities arrived in Marshall to arrest him, he was already dead and buried. They seized the mansion for debts and thus the curse of Abner Pratt began. My suspicions about the small grave stone were finally being realized now that I saw he had died penniless. It left a big part of me wondering, as I gazed up to the large stone bearing the name Gorham, if perhaps Abner and his family had been given those plots out of kindness? Maybe the stones were paid for by the Gotham family instead. Perhaps the banker knew where the rest of the money went? No proof that there was any shadier business going on, but certainly something to think about.

Also, I should mention that authorities did visit Pratt at the mansion while it was being built following suspicion that monies were missing on his account. He insisted to them that he had no money. Without trying to trace down how he was building the mansion without any money, they instead closed their investigation completely.

The home has had four private owners in its lifetime, not including the Historical Society. Over the years it became dilapidated and worn to the point of almost no repair. It is believed by some that there was a curse upon the house since Abner Pratt had likely used bad money to build it and eventually, in time, caught up with the very walls as they crumbled to the ground.

Another story states that one owner had to sell off two of the wings of the house to pay to keep it going, while another replaced all the marble fireplaces with faux ones to have money. One owner's daughter even went mad, eating glass and curtains in the mansion. And still another owner was left widowed extremely early in life. Were these merely coincidences? All and all, by the end it was evident that even the grand Honolulu House could no longer hold the secrets of the Hawaiian scandal. Time, and a nagging plague of misfortune, had worn it to shreds as it stood to await its final bow. Abner Pratt's final curtain was closing on all the terror he had inflicted until one man reversed it all.

Mr. Harold Brooks was born in 1885 and his claim to fame and fortune was the invention of the Brooks Rupture Appliance, a hernia truss. It was touted as the most comfortable truss available and he made a great sum of money manufacturing and selling it. Brooks was also a true preservationist and philanthropist, donating much of his time and money to the city of Marshall. He owned over a dozen historical structures, saving them from the wrecking ball.

One such cornerstone was the Honolulu House which was left to perish, taking its twisted and tangled history along with it. The mansion was said to be on the brink of being torn down and replaced with a gas station when Harold purchased it and saved a town treasure. It is said that this was the day the curse was lifted and the home regained its intended beauty through the hands of someone who banished the wrong that had built its walls.

To this day, it stands as a reminder of the greed of men. For me, it is a memory of those who suffered at the hands of Abner Pratt. His legacy may be tarnished, but perhaps he can rest now that his story has been told.

Over the years the Honolulu house has had several paranormal occurrences and has even been investigated professionally. Here are a few of the accounts surrounding this cornerstone of Marshall history.

Carrie Cameron

The Cameron family owned the Honolulu house and are responsible for the "stairway that goes to nowhere". Well, not exactly nowhere, but it is a grand staircase that ends at a small little porch at the top of the home. It was built for the owner's daughter, Carrie, to come down on her wedding day. Carrie's wedding gown is also on display at the museum. Newly wedded couples who are photographed in and around the home often end up with an "extra" person in their photo, especially on the stairs. Carrie has been said to have made many cameos in photos over the years. She continues to be attracted to the Honolulu House, perhaps since her wedding was one of the best days of her life!

Jessie Graham

Jessie Graham, a descendant of the famed fugitive slave Adam Crosswhite, was the servant of Annette Bouliard, who also owned the mansion at one point in history. Now Jessie was no ordinary servant and she developed a deeper relationship with her boss than just that of an employee. Ms. Bouliard became almost like an adopted mom and even educated Ms. Graham. Jessie was said to have been very fond of her time here in Marshall and, as you can imagine, her odd life as so much more than a worker. She especially enjoyed baking in the basement kitchen. Today, the essence of fresh bread and sweets can sometimes be smelled in or around the kitchen and it is said that Jessie is still working away in the home she loved so well! Guests have even commented on the delicious aromas only to find out the kitchen hasn't worked in decades!

I was told once by a previous director that they had brought some Civil War relics to the museum to be catalogued. Subsequently, the experiences she began to witness compelled her to have a professional paranormal investigation done, much to the dismay of the board. Nevertheless, she had several odd things happen while the items were in custody. The elevator suddenly began to open and shut and go floor to floor. Several times it was inspected for any sort of electrical defect. Even after being repaired, the elevator would go from floor to floor.

At one point, things got rather personal when she was putting Christmas decorations on the tree. An entire box of bulbs was thrown across the room from the ladder breaking against the far wall.

During the investigation, a medium told her that there was a man attached to some of the newly arrived items in the home, specifically a Civil war sword. The man was not a fan of Christmas nor did he approve of women who wore pants. The items were packed up and sent down the road to the GAR Museum, which specialized in Civil War artifacts. The hauntings ceased immediately.

The Honolulu House remains an intricate part of what Marshall is today and what she was in the past. It is a reflection of both challenges in the human psych and triumphs in conscious goodness. Unraveling the mystery behind its true origins may be bleak but the truth of its existence today marks one man's journey (Mr. Brooks) into saving a piece of living history and a community's faith that others will want to relish in the stories that surround its existence, no matter the position. It is unlikely you will hear any of these stories on your visit, but rest assured, the main attraction and life of Abner Pratt is but a Google away if you so choose to research on your own!

I should also mention, in closing, that a few select individuals have passed down the oral story that perhaps Charles Gorham actually had a hand in tipping off the bounty hunters and slave owner in order to gain some notoriety for an already lacking Marshall, with the hopes of drawing in more residents to invest in such a "forward thinking" city. A city that truly freed slaves and kept them safe, no matter the cost. It would make perfect sense since Gorham was in finance, owning a private bank in Marshall until 1865 wherein he incorporated the institution to First National Bank of Marshall and served as president until his retirement in 1898. Seems as though the idea was that he created this stir in order to bring national attention. If you are the sort that follows the money then this theory could be interesting to say the least.

Oakridge Cemetery

Touted as the second oldest cemetery in Michigan with its official inception in 1839, it stems back much further, even at its current location which was begun in 1835. This makes it technically the oldest cemetery in Michigan, although it wasn't incorporated as such. A minor technicality. Also, it should be noted that the original cemetery was located on the Southwestern section of town by Green and Hanover Streets, which was later moved to its current location. All of the people we talk about in this book are likely buried there.

It is comprised of sixty-five acres hosting over 11,000 deceased residents. That is a pretty big place for a small community of around 7,000. Currently, there are more people dead in Marshall than alive and that isn't even counting St. Mary's Cemetery on Michigan Avenue just west of town. That is also not considering the unknown number of bodies buried in various yards from way 'back

in the day.' It certain does give one a sense though, of how many people have been through here and how populated it was at different points in history.

Most times, in my general experience, cemeteries only have paranormal activity on a rare basis. We have a handful of legends, if you will, that have been orally told over the years. The setting of Oakridge is really like a park and it is common to see people riding bikes, jogging and walking their dogs. It is pristine, peaceful and as my kids would say, where all my friends are.

After school, they would ask to drive through and say hello to all the people we talk about on our ghost tours.

They believe that their dad, me, keeps their stories alive. Many days you could find me alone, or with my wife on nice days, looking at gravestones or riding a horse and buggy listening to the stories in the wind, just being with those who I have spent several years getting to know. Somewhere inside, when I haven't been in a while, I think they miss me and long for my return for whatever that is worth. I like to visit the people I have come to know at Oakridge and it gives me some sort of peace knowing that they aren't forgotten.

Lt. George A. Woodruff

As you turn into the main entrance of the cemetery you will be greeted with the vault containing the last resting place of 1st Lieutenant George A. Woodruff. He died July 4th, 1863 after being mortally wounded during Pickett's Charge on July 3rd at Gettysburg. The story goes that after his parents found out about his death, his mother was so distraught that his father went all the way down to Gettysburg to personally deliver his sons body back home. This vault is where they had previously put people who died in the winter until spring. Then the ground could be dug up and they would then be buried. It is very large and Lt Woodruff is the only body interned within. It is chained and padlocked and the keys to the tomb are with someone in Woodruff's family. People have said

they have heard the bars of the gate to the tomb rattle and have heard moans, groans and mumbling noises coming from within the tomb. It is a great place to capture photos of orbs and strange light anomalies.

The Shadow Man

There are a few tales in Oakridge and one is that of The Shadow Man, Mr. Boughton. Located in the old section on the southeast far corner is a gravestone that stands with a picture of a scroll on it that shines at night when lights hit it.

It was said that back in the 1970's someone did a pictorial of the cemetery, taking pictures of each section one by one. When the film was developed, the photographer noticed that there appeared to be a shadow of a man standing behind the Boughton family stone. Legend quickly sparked and for the last forty years, seekers of the paranormal have ventured out taking pictures they hope would capture the shadow of a ghost! We do not know who, exactly, he was in life. We have toured this site on several occasions and have taken at least six questionable photos, including one that appears to have a white shadow of a woman next to the dark shadow. It seems that the second figure is screaming with her mouth open. The individual who took the picture refused to give it up as it upset him gravely and gave him an eerie feeling.

Crying Mary

Across the two-track dirt trail, from the Boughtons, is a statue of a goddess of sorts that has been dubbed the "Crying Mary". This is not a statue of the Virgin Mary. Mary appears to be the first name given to the person buried there. Many have said that 'Mary' cries for the one buried. The statue has stains at the base of the eyes and there are many locals who claim to have witnessed actual tears flowing from them. Also, we should mention, that there have been  reports of the sound of a crying child near a bush about twenty feet from the statue. Whether the incidents are related is unknown but the entire area is full of paranormal experiences.

The Dawnwalker

Near the back of the cemetery is the sad story of the Dawnwalker. She is said to be a young woman dressed in a 1970's/80's pea coat who walks from the middle to the very back of the cemetery disappearing amongst some graves. Upon further investigation, we were told that this was the ghost of a woman who had died in a tragic accident in the 1980's. She was with a group of friends on a boating trip and a storm came up on Lake Michigan. The boat capsized and two of the women drowned. The legend goes on to relate that one woman's body, the Dawnwalker, walks the length of the cemetery to a lonely grave that bears her name. Some even say her body was never recovered and that the apparition is searching for the spot of her eternal resting place. I have personally met many people, including staff members and tour takers, who have witnessed seeing this apparition. The young lady may have reached a tragic end, but her story is still told and in some regard, she lives with each passing person that searches for her.

The Lonely Graves at Pauper's Field

Pauper's or Potter's Field, located at the rear of the cemetery, while appearing fairly empty is filled with bodies. The majority of those buried here do not have a head stone because this is the area where people buried their dead for little or no cost. Most of the bodies are from the mid-1800s when Marshall had a large train stop. When people died on the train they were buried at the next station, which, on occasion, was Marshall. Illness was common while traveling on the trains during that time because of tight quarters and poor sanitation. There are numerous children buried here who died of colds and pneumonia while on their travels. They never made it home while parents and relatives left their loved ones far from home. This is also a place of high activity and picture taking is a must!

Adam Crosswhite, the fugitive slave

In 1843, Adam and his family were on a plantation in Kentucky. They ran away because the slave owner, Francis Giltner, told Adam that he was going to sell Adam's four children and separate the family. Marshall was one of the last stops on the underground railroad before Canada. At that time, Marshall was a very progressive town. There were small cabins built on the outskirts of town for slave families that decided to stay in Marshall, instead of continuing on to Canada. They were afforded whatever protection the community could offer.

Adam and his family decided to stay in Marshall. The Crosswhite family was in town for a few years before their slave owner found them. One night, in December 1846, the Crosswhites heard a pounding on their door and voices demanding they come out. The Crosswhites hid inside their home. It was the voice of Francis Toutman, a nephew of Giltner and two other men who had been hired to return the family to slavery.

It is said that their neighbor, commonly known as old black Sam, used to go around town every morning ringing a bell, telling the news for the day. When he saw what was happening to the Crosswhites, perhaps signaled from Adam's warning shot from a rifle, he got his bell and he went around town telling people what was going on.

Very shortly there were about 200-300 people surrounding the home. The townspeople were saying that the slave owner was trespassing on private property and convinced a deputy to arrest him. Ironically, it was a deputy sheriff that was paid by Toutman to pose as a census enumerator in order to locate the family.

A reputable businessman about the town, Charles Gorham, reportedly held a town meeting in which the men were charged with assault, battery and house breaking, thus held for two days. The townspeople used this time to get the Crosswhite family on a carriage and on their way to Canada.

The slave owner federally sued Charles Gorham for "stealing his property" and he won a sum of $4,800. (at the time, you could build one of the huge mansions in town for around $5,000). Upon paying the fee, it was stated that

a slave would never be given back in Marshall.

After the Civil War was over and slavery was truly abolished, the Crosswhite family came back to Marshall to live because they said it was the only place they really felt welcomed. Adam and four of his relatives are buried in his plot, while one of his children is buried in an unknown grave in the old section. People have captured images of a man and little boy standing over this grave holding hands. It is believed to be Adam Crosswhite and one of his sons.

Civil War and Oakridge Legends

The Civil war section is also a high activity area and boasts a host of great picture opportunities.

It is also interesting to mention the legend of John Wilkes Booth and the idea that he may or may not be buried at Oakridge Cemetery. This is a story I have heard countless times by visitors, Civil War and Lincoln enthusiasts alike and I have never been able to make the correlation except for the fact that Lincoln is buried at an Oakridge Cemetery in Illinois. Also, there is a legend that the actual Booth was not killed or that he did not get buried where we have been told. It is interesting that part of this legend attached itself to Marshall and certainly worth mentioning.

The Witch of Marshall

One last note is that over the years, from several locals, had been told the story of a gravestone that supposedly vanished. The stone was in the old section near the back and was inscribed with nothing other than: Here Lies a Witch. I have not been able to verify any sort of resource that would lead me to have concrete evidence that there were ever witches in Marshall, but it is completely plausible.

The cemetery itself is a hotspot for photographic oddities such as the infamous orbs. I have seen everything photographed from shadow figures to fine mists that appeared, including full body apparitions. I have witnessed batteries die and electronics fail on tours, along with drops in temperature that are clearly definitive. Employed tour guides have experienced our horses getting spooked and not wanting to travel in certain sections on countless trips as well. Over the years more and more photos have been taken of the paranormal at Oakridge. It was told to me by a well-known medium who visited, that the spirits have enjoyed us talking about them and bringing people out to see them on a regular basis. I urge you to take a trip to visit some of my friends when you get the chance and perhaps they will reveal themselves to you as well.

Does Zenos Tillotson Haunt The Stagecoach Inn?

There is a presence that lingers from days gone-by downtown at the infamous Stagecoach Inn. It is that of its first proprietor, Zenos Tillotson, or so it has been presumed. Built in 1838, it is the oldest continuously operated inn on the Detroit to Chicago stagecoach line, and today operates as a local pub boasting the best burger in Southwest Michigan. Locals and visitors alike have been patronizing this establishment for many generations and most know about the legends and paranormal, especially if they ever lived or worked there. This Greek Revival building is one of a kind in its downtown setting and is clearly a focal point of the Main Street of Marshall. It has survived the test of time and has been the resting place of many weary travelers.

A few stories linger in and around the "Coach" and sometimes the line between seeing spirits and consuming spirits can be fuzzy. One such tale is of the Underground

Railroad and the role the building played as a stopping point as the slaves made their way to freedom in Canada. It has been said that there are (or were) hidden rooms and even a tunnel that led toward Schuler's Restaurant across Eagle St. through a faux fireplace. Also, it is said that a secret room existed under where the sidewalk is today on the Michigan Avenue side that allowed people to hide out. It is well-known as a landmark representing the escape of the slaves who fled the South.

For the people who have lived upstairs, strange sounds can sometimes be heard as if someone in boots is walking down halls. Normally, the sound ends just before the apartment door and when occupants have gazed out their peep hole, they see nothing. Sometimes, along with the footsteps, it sounds as if someone is carrying a case of empty, clanging bottles.

For the workers downstairs, the tales continue. I have heard repeatedly from many past and present employees that they have had their own share of odd happenings. Most of the stories revolve around closing time when the girls report the feeling of someone pulling at their hair or the juke box turning on without prompting. They've also heard footsteps and clanging bottles from the back hall which leads to the restrooms and offices.

As I have spent a great amount of time in Marshall wandering its story-lined streets, I have a few of my own experiences, one of which was at The Stagecoach Inn. I was standing at the bar as I had many times before. Owning the tour business next door, I would come over for change on occasion. As I stood there talking with the bartender and a local guy who was in for a drink, all the glasses started to rattle. It wasn't unusual for them to do this when a semi-truck passed by. This time was much different.

First, there was no semi and second, one of the shot glasses sprang from behind the bar and landed in the dish sink about three feet away. All three of us were stunned, silent and questioning what we had just witnessed. Nervous chuckles filled the room. Still, to this day, I wonder if what I saw was real or if, by chance, I made it all up in my head Then again, I may have witnessed something beyond my comprehension as minute as it may have been.

Another puzzling story is one from the owner who called me and said they had witnessed a fog of some kind which was caught on the security camera. They could watch as it made its way down the bar before vanishing. Although the owners are skeptical, they did have some questions that were left unanswered by this event.

This is obviously a public building and very accessible to visit, affording the opportunity to perhaps have your own experience. Whether it is the ghost of Zenos Tillotson or that of a weary traveler that decided to stay, The Stagecoach Inn remains a gathering place to have and meet some great spirits!

Historically, there are also several rumors, as you may imagine, surrounding this structure. It is stated that Abraham Lincoln made a speech from the front balcony at one point on his campaign trail. Al Capone supposedly rented the front suite when he visited the Purple Gang from Detroit and met them in Albion, a neighboring city. Throughout its rich history The Stagecoach Inn stands as a landmark of hospitality.

The Lady in Red and a Host of Rattlings at the National House Inn

Meeting the owner of the Inn, as anyone who has met her can testify, is a sure delight. She is truly one of a kind with a grace and hospitality that invites you to feel welcome. I had the chance to meet with her when my business opened back in 2009. I was excited to hear, first hand, her little collection of stories of perhaps the most famous ghosts residing in Marshall. She has owned the inn for some forty years now and has seen a plethora of visitors interested in 'that which goes bump in the night' behind her walls. While she doesn't advertise her Bed and Breakfast as haunted, she knows the legends that lure some to her doorstep and, on occasion, will delight a customer in her knowledge of the unknown. I was lucky enough to get that chance.

The Inn was built in 1835 by Colonel Andrew Mann and was known as Mann's Hotel. In 1878, after the railroad rush in Marshall, it became a factory called *Windmills and*

Wagons. By 1902, the tide had turned yet again and it was turned into luxury apartments known as Dean's Flats. After nearly seventy-five years, it in fell into disrepair and the clientele were anything but luxurious. Luckily, in 1976, it was reopened, completely remodeled, once again as an inn.

Today it is a beautifully successful B&B. Over the years, it has been a place of rest for many souls on journeys across the land as well as a hotspot for the Underground Railroad, complete with a hidden room attached to the phone booth for extra security. Not your everyday place and certainly full of stories-- if only the walls could talk.

I was privileged to get my own private interview and discussion of the paranormal right from the owner. She told me that even before she purchased the inn in the 1970's, it had been studied by a group of paranormal investigators from the University of Michigan, wherein they confirmed some of the stories and events that follow and continue to this day.

In the room known as The Blue Room one can, occasionally, smell two distinct odors that seemingly manifest from its walls: Smoke and a heavy floral perfume. This is believed to be the spirits of perhaps a couple that decided to keep their residence even in death.

The next phenomenon is the sound of a firing gun that resonates and follows with the sound of a door slamming which is rumored to be the ghost of a man who was shot right out the door, falling dead on Michigan Ave.

Another, more in-depth tale, is that of a little boy who has been seen wandering upstairs and hanging out on the front staircase. He has even at times spoken to visitors and says his name is Jason. He is always described as a young boy in period clothes from the 1800's. One couple was so distraught after speaking with Jason that they went to the owner to state their concern and the fact that he had told them he just wanted people to see him.

Likely the most controversial and talked about story is that of the Lady in Red who is presumed to be the spirit of a woman of the night or, at the very least, someone of questionable company. She is responsible, it is said, for hiding women's clothes and jewelry along with appearing in the upper windows and hallways. Many guests and residents of town claim to have caught a glimpse of her and some even speculate on who she actually is. I have heard she is a relative from many residents who want to claim her. The story has stretched and stretched throughout time, but one thing remains true ... all accounts are that of a woman in a red dress.

I had the opportunity to have a guest on a historical tour a few years back and was told quite an interesting story regarding the Lady in Red with one of his employees. It was the oil spill of 2011 and Marshall was flooded with people working on the pipeline. The hotels and inns were packed, leaving no room for visitors most nights for what seemed to be forever.

The supervisor told me that his employee came to work one day after staying at The National House Inn. His face was, quite literally, as pale as a ghost! When asked, the employee told the story of how he awoke at 4am to a woman in a red dress straddling him in bed with her face just inches from his, staring into his eyes. He claimed that the two stared at each other for many seconds before she vanished. He said he could even feel the weight of her body on his. He quickly packed his belongings and left petrified and refused to stay there again. The supervisor had to find him different lodging and was interested to know if a woman in a red dress had ever been reported. Of course, I indulged him.

That was the story that validated, in my mind, all that I had heard from folks in town. I had finally gotten an eyewitness that wasn't aware of the legend. To me it was credible and left me questioning what really happened. Was the Lady in Red reliving her profession with a single man who lying in bed helplessly? How many stories are there like this? None that I know of, but after much thought, how many single men have stayed at this B&B over the years? How many would admit to such a tale? Likely this was her opportunity rarely afforded in her afterlife.

The National House Inn is still in operation and is an exquisite place to stay whether you are on a ghost hunt, a friend weekend or a romantic getaway. The staff are friendly and if you are lucky enough, one of them may slip and tell you a story that will rattle your bones and make sleeping a bit difficult. Guests, both living and dead, continue to stay at the little inn on the roundabout and the stories and legends will grow and prosper into new generations of inquisitive folks.

Shorter Bumps in the Night

The 3am Knocker and The Little Girl

Downtown, above Sullivan's Insurance Agency, there are a few entities that make themselves known on occasion. It is said that at 3 in the morning, there comes a knock by one such spirit on the apartment doors. When residents answer, there is no one in sight. There is also a little girl that appears at the top of the stairs and quickly vanishes when she is spotted. Stop in and ask for yourself. The Sullivan family is sure to have a tale to spin!

Buried in the Backyard

A family lived at a home on Exchange Street for more than 30 years. They raised their two sons there and throughout their childhoods, both sons reported seeing a little boy with no legs floating around their room. Not only was this an odd thing for a child to imagine, but what made it more curious, was that the boys both came to their mom at different times and each separately reported seeing the little boy. Growing up, both boys witnessed the apparition on multiple occasions.

This property is about five city lots deep and for many years much of the backyard was unkept. Several years ago, when the children were grown, the owners had professional gardens put in throughout the back of the property. When the workers were clearing brush from the lot, they found a lonely head stone for a six-year-old boy named Eugene Cane. No other grave markers were ever found and no other information about the boy is known. It was an eerie connection nonetheless.

The Octagon House

This home is one of few octagon houses in the area and was built in 1856. The current owners found hidden rooms in the basement when they moved here several years ago. The rooms are believed to be those used during the days of the Underground Railroad. They have reportedly heard murmurs and banging noises from below and assume they are echoes of the slaves that may

have hidden there for their safety. It is a residual energy that comes and goes.

Currently the Octagon House is being restored after many years of neglect.

Schuler's Restaurant

Albert Schuler, famed restauranteur, lived in an apartment on the third floor of his beloved Schuler's Restaurant and, as rumors go, it has been completely preserved to look just like the day he left it. It is cleaned by the staff, but nothing is moved. Employees have often reported smelling cigar smoke in the kitchen and have received complaints from customers about a cigar smell as well. Albert is also known to play tricks on the employees, doing things like flushing all the toilets simultaneously while they are cleaning the restrooms, especially in the one above Winston's, a quaint pub

attached with outdoor seating, named after his son. A fine place to eat and perhaps an unexpected visit from the original chef himself will add to your dining experience.

Michigan's First Governor's Mansion

This home was built in 1839 by J. Gordon, who was elected lieutenant governor of Michigan in 1840, and became acting governor in 1841. During this time, it was believed that Marshall would become the state capitol, however; in the early 40s, Marshall lost that vote (by one as rumor has it) to Lansing, known as the Red Cedar District. Gordon, along with many others left the area.

The mansion is now a museum operated by the Daughters of the American Revolution and is haunted by at least a couple of entities. Guests are welcome during visiting hours and in recent years, the museum has even hosted some paranormal events, much to the contrary of other local museums, who tend to shy away from attracting ghost enthusiasts.

The first spirit is that of a little girl who is seen standing in the service stairwell. She quickly disappears once she is spotted and is said to have arrived after some relics were dug up from the yard.

In a town like Marshall, if you want to know more about the people who lived in a specific home, the best place to dig would be where the outhouse was located. People not only used it as a toilet but also as a place to throw unwanted items. They did just that at the Governor's Mansion, digging and unearthing several items. It was after this excavation that this little girl started making her appearance, thus accounting for paranormal happenings that are attached to items rather than an individual residence.

There is also an older woman who is known to pace around the bedroom upstairs and mess up the bed. It is thought to be the ghost of Mrs. Gordon or so she has been named by various mediums who have visited. Throughout the years, employees of the museum have sworn that the sheets had just been neat, but when they looked again, they were wrinkled like someone had been sitting there. A real piece of Michigan history and a fun place to visit for the whole family … take your camera in case you run into either of these spirits! The staff is warm and friendly and full of fun so be sure to ask about their guests from the other side!

Stonehall…The Flynn Family Secret

Okay, there are always a few legends that might be so far out there that they could be true or perhaps just a twisted version of several stories. Or perhaps none of it happened at all. That is the case of home nicknamed Stonehall on North Kalamazoo. I am not certain where this story started or to whom it owes its credit, but there have been many different individuals who have claimed it true on separate accounts. It is the story of the Flynn family secret. A well-known family with a twisted tale of murder and deceit.

It is said that Mr. Flynn had taken up a long-time affair with the housekeeper. It is thought that perhaps Mrs. Flynn knew of the indiscretions, but turned a blind eye. However, it was evident that the housekeeper had

become pregnant and since she had no suitor, Mr. Flynn was likely the father.

One day, while the pregnant housekeeper was atop the stairway, she fell mysteriously to her death, thus killing the baby relieving the Flynns from the burden of that atrocity. Although the evidence was gone, the town murmured of the death and rumors began to fly, calling for murder. It was a widely held thought that Mrs. Flynn had somehow been involved in the demise of the housekeeper, but no charges were ever brought up. Eventually the Flynn family secret turned to yet another legend passed from generation to generation.

Many owners of the home have supposedly witnessed the apparition of a young woman at the top of the stairs who falls to her death into a mangled pile at the bottom before vanishing. This is a repetitive haunting and many who have seen her have offered her help by telling her she didn't have to jump but to no avail; she succumbs anyhow. I am not sure how this story came to be, but it has intrigued locals for many years and continues to be a mystery.

Hung up at the First Fire House

The garage to this home on Exchange St. across from the Governor's Mansion is Marshall's first fire house. During the time that this location was in operation, each family in town would pay $5 per year to the fire department. They were then given a number to put above their front door. This was done so that the fire department knew that the family had paid their dues should there ever be a fire in that home.

If you did have a fire and you had not paid your fee that year, then the fire department would not put your fire out or they would charge you a hefty fee! At this point in time, their "fire truck" was a horse drawn vehicle filled with water. When news came that there was a fire in town, the firemen would have to harness and hitch all the horses. Considering the number of oil lamps in the homes and the amount of flammable material, you would have been lucky if the fire department arrived in time to save any part of your burning home regardless of your payment.

There is an unrelated haunting in this old garage. People have reported walking into the garage and catching a glimpse of a man hanging from a noose in the rafters. Previous owners of this home and even a woman who was driving by while the garage door was open have reported seeing this. It is said that the driver of the car even called 911 to report what she had seen. According to local legend during the mid-1900s there was a hanging suicide at this location.

The Ghost of Harold Brooks

This is one of the many homes bought and preserved by Harold Brookes. This one was his home. It stands erected on the Northeastern corner of Kalamazoo and Prospect Streets. It is a beautiful Greek Revival and is currently under renovation. According to local legend, there used to be a tunnel that connected this home to Stonehall across N. Kalamazoo Ave. The tunnel no longer exists, however the entrance to the tunnel remains in the basement of the Brooks home. Many debates on this tunnel have occurred between the citizens of Marshall on whether it ever existed. The tunnel was supposedly a means to transport slaves from house to house during the Underground Railroad days. To this day it is not uncommon to hear about the tunnel when talking with a local about these homes.

A woman in town who lived here for a short time, several years ago, claims that on two separate occasions she saw a man appear in different parts of the house briefly, then disappear. She described the man as well kept, wearing a white suit. She convinced herself that her visions were just her mind playing tricks on her, until a few months later when she was cleaning out the basement and found an old photo album. The photos were worn, but she could clearly see several of the pictures, including one of a man in a white suit; the same man she had seen appear in the house previously. The man was Harold Brooks.

The Cronin House

This home was built by Jeremiah Cronin, a local business owner, in 1872. His two granddaughters, Virginia and Elizabeth both resided in the home until their deaths. Neither ever married and they lived together their whole lives. They even adopted a son. Unfortunately, he died as a young man during war and the Cronin sisters were said to become completely reclusive following his death. They spent all their time in the home and scarcely socialized or

had visitors. The sisters have been seen by passersby standing in the second story, looking out the window. In fact, a few years ago one of our customers took this photo of the home during a tour and later realized there were a few figures staring out between the curtains. Another former owner of the home had informed us that the bed

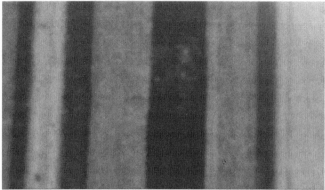

sheets would be pulled off him and his wife during the night and that strange noises were heard throughout the home; however, he didn't reside there long enough for any more stories.

It is also the setting for the famed book by John Bellairs, renowned and award-winning author, *The House with a Clock in its Walls*. It has stirred curiosity from locals and visitors alike as it is shrouded in mystery. It is always one of the top houses to visit for this very reason.

Jacks Upstairs

There is even a home on North Kalamazoo that is well known to have a little boy who can be heard playing Jacks upstairs. It's a small story but also indicative of the fact that Marshall has so many stories, that even the smallest deserve some moment of relevance to the entire picture. There are literally dozens and dozens of these that add to the overall ambience of the paranormal experience that is Marshall.

The Little Boy at The Marshall House Inn

The Marshall House Inn, currently Shops at The Marshall House was built in the late 1830s / early 1840s as a grand hotel. The original building took up an entire city block and included forty-four suites, restaurants and shops. The current structure is only about 1/8 of its original size. Shortly after Marshall lost the vote for the state capitol, the Inn closed as people were no longer traveling to Marshall nearly as much as before and the it could no longer sustain itself. After its closure, a smaller, much more modest hotel was built just west a block down Michigan Ave., where the Post Office stands today. It was called the Hernden Hotel. It ran successfully for about ten years until one night an oil lamp tipped over and started a fire. The fire spread rapidly, killing many of the customers and employees that were in the fully booked hotel. Within twenty minutes, the fire had ravaged almost the entire building. Newspaper articles of the event recount horrible scenes of people jumping from windows and attempting to throw their loved ones to safety.

At the time, the Marshall House was sitting vacant just a block away and the town's people decided to use the empty building as a triage station of sorts, as the story goes. Most of the victims who were brought to the old Inn died from their injuries.

As the events unfold, one of those people was a little boy, the grandson of a house keeper working at the hotel that night. Today, people report seeing a young boy standing in the most eastern second-story window of the Marshall

House facing Michigan Ave. Sightings of this boy have been reported by many gas station and hospital employees who use the small park outside the building for breaks. Most witnesses state that they see the boy in the middle of the night or very early morning hours.

Previous owners of the building have also claimed to walk in the building and smell smoke on numerous occasions, though there is no fire or apparent source of the smell. The building was also a funeral home with living quarters upstairs for a time. Certainly, a tragic story and perhaps the reason a soul or two was left behind to wander lost for eternity.

Tunnels Everywhere

Many legends and rumors abound the city of tunnels that were part of the Underground Railroad missions. Many residents insist that not only do a few homes possess tunnels connecting them, but many of the buildings on the roundabout also were connected to move people from place to place below ground. The main places in question would be the National House Bed and Breakfast, the Honolulu House and what today is Chemical Bank. It creates a division in Marshall between fact and fiction and even though the Underground Railroad wasn't actually underground, it still makes this a great mystery. There are residents who swear they have seen the doors in basements and that the oral tale is truth. I am skeptical, but remain entranced by the origin of these stories and assume that, perhaps, it is at least part fact.

Hannah and The Oliver Comstock House

There is a home on the corner of Green and Exchange Streets which holds a more current ghastly tale, which most locals have had or known witnesses of paranormal happenings. It is known as the Comstock house or more affectionately, The Hannah House. I will try my best to unravel this tale based on several eye witness accounts, and local lore.

The home was built by Oliver Comstock in the 1830's. Oliver was a Renaissance man of sorts being everything from a Doctor and Lawyer to a Clergyman. He was also a big part of the Patent Medicine industry that briefly swept through Marshall. He had a wife named Hanna and this is partly her story.

In the 1980's, a family moved into the Comstock house. The story is that the husband and wife were expecting their second child and the wife, when picking out names for the baby, had become certain that the name should be Hannah, with an "h" at the end. It was neither a family name nor one they ever considered before living in the new house. The baby was born and thus the name Hannah was given and she began one of the most recent ghost adventures in Marshall. She awakened something within the house that would not be silenced during their stay.

Hannah was only a few weeks old at the first paranormal happening. It was a normal night of slumber when the parents awoke to the pounding of their piano downstairs in the front  entryway. The husband bolted to his feet and began his journey cautiously to where the noise was coming from.

As he flipped the light on in the stairwell the piano instantly ceased its incessant noise. He made his way to the piano and much to his surprise, there wasn't a sign of any foul play. He turned to check the rest of the house. Upon reaching the hallway, he noticed, written in pencil on the wall, the name Hanna without the "h". Seeing how their children were far too young to have done this, and the fact that neither he nor his wife claimed responsibility, it appeared to be something unexplainable, of the paranormal. The family, from that day forward experienced a presence unlike anything they had ever witnessed before or would again.

Over the years strange things occurred at the Comstock house and our story blends true accounts by family and friends with local lore that has been, I'm sure, stretched and molded into what it is today. Rumors and legends surrounding this home have run rampant and there are several takes on this story. The family is said to have experienced seeing a woman gazing from the front upstairs window on occasion and experiencing everything from strange writings on the walls to doors opening and shutting.

Even actual contact between Hannah and a woman from the other side existed. Members of the house had even been said to be lightly "pushed" down the stairs at times. Friends of the children stated that they would not hang out at the house and would, instead, request the children to play at their home because of the eerie feelings and events they would witness.

Even though this is a relatively new story, it does become muddled and rides a thin line between what is fact and what is a game of telephone, where the tale has been added and subtracted to as it has been told. Most interestingly, it is claimed that the family, after years of living in the home, decided to dig a pool on the side of the house only to uncover three bodies. Two of the bodies were said to be of children and the third, a woman, Hanna Comstock, Oliver's first wife. It was customary to have family cemeteries at one's home. The bodies were moved and thus settling the mystery of whom their spirits were, however; the paranormal events continued.

The family opened a Bed and Breakfast at the home and had several complaints about odd noises and occasional knocks on guest's doors in the middle of the night with no one held responsible. One couple stayed and was getting ready for the night with the wife in the bathroom and the man lying on the bed reading in his underwear. It is said that the bed lifted several inches in the air before slamming to the ground. The man ran down the stairs and was seen by the owners standing on the sidewalk in front of the house scared out of his mind.

The children grew as all normally do and the home eventually became too big for the family. They moved and to my knowledge the home has never had a single paranormal event since. The family has also never experienced any more hauntings after leaving. No matter what truth lies within this story, I am certain that the family, especially Hannah, will always remember her time spent experiencing the other side.

The home sat vacant for quite some time before a new family purchased it and many people have claimed it possessed a strange vibe. It was eventually sold for much less than it was worth. Currently, it is seeing much needed renovations and restoration. The couple there did inform me that even though they believed none of the stories surrounding the house, they did find an old brochure from a Marshall Home Tour and when they opened it, the name Hanna was written inside. Perhaps a sign that she is still around. Whatever the facts, this home remains one of the most talked about paranormal destinations and there are several people in town who have their own recollection of experiences surrounding the events that took place.

The Cronin Building

Built in 1852, the majestic Cronin has always been a cornerstone of the downtown arena as she towers above, her windows capturing, like a timeless camera, the comings and goings of over a hundred fifty years of Marshall traffic. It was within her walls that I opened my first store back in 2010. What a grand treat it was and an extremely exciting time. I wasn't quite prepared for the paranormal inhabitants, nor their peculiar behavior, but it lent itself well to the final understanding of this journey.

It was only about a week into cleaning and preparations to open when my friend and I were staying late, burning the midnight oil sweeping and relentlessly organizing, when we heard our first voice. There was a sound of a man clearing his throat and then a resounding "may I help you" that followed. We were dumbfounded, completely taken aback and halted in our endeavors for the evening. For the entire time I spent within this location I encountered many unexplainable actions and this voice was a prominent happening.

It was not only myself that heard the voice but others who had lingered long enough in my shop, including friends and relatives. Many of my female employees had been touched on the shoulder or had their hair tugged while going down the stairs to the restroom in the basement. I, along with others, had doors slam, lights turn off, heard thuds that echoed from the upper levels and what seemed to sound like someone shuffling their feet above. One person explained that it was one of the Cronin sisters, Virginia or Elizabeth, using their cane and still making

her way through what would have been her apartment in life. A group of us even collectively attended a paranormal investigation and saw a door upstairs fly off of the hinges and land on one of the participants. The activity was extremely high during these days and paved the way for much of my inspiration into the paranormal.

The building itself possessed a type of longing for the reckoning of Marshall within many of us around at that time, an almost calling to delve into something deeper than ourselves, trapping us. We were mesmerized by her glory even in decay. Her cracks and creaks held a special place in our hearts and we found solace there as we dreamt of our next move in this sleepy little town. It was a time of great persona leaps of consciousness and a semblance of believers who saw something invigorating in the energy we were creating. It's gone now, like a drifting smoke, but the memories remain and those of us who still talk, come together to bathe in the knowing that we experienced something beyond what we ever dreamed.

Today there are plans to open the grand Cronin once again. This time as a restaurant with apartments upstairs. I remember quite clearly when the current owner came to my shop to ask me about the hauntings of the building. He and his crew, from what I understand, have witnessed many of the same peculiar happenings as we did years ago. Ironically, they have decided to name the restaurant Two Sisters, which is sure to conjure up more activity and perhaps some surprise visits to their patrons and staff.

123 W. Prospect Street

Having the chance to purchase and live in a haunted house is really a luck of the draw, except when you live in Marshall. I have had the opportunity to live in two-- Prospect St. being the most recent. Built as early as the 1850's, this quaint shotgun cottage is a real gem and a hit at home tour, which is held yearly as people open up their homes to visitors. It is a two to three bedroom that is about fourteen-foot-wide and two stories. It is painted red, white and blue. Nestled between a larger home and another cottage style home, one barely has room to turn around inside, but what it lacks in size it most certainly makes up for in

charm. It didn't take long before we realized there was more than met the eye to the stories told. I tried to scoff it off around our young boys, but following are the accounts of our experiences.

There were clearly two entities present: One of a child, the other clearly an adult male. The child could be heard running around upstairs. When it was quiet, we would listen to the steps of little feet across the ceiling and up and down the stairs as well. We lost two babysitters at that house because of the apparitions. Both times, the sitters claimed that the boys were in bed and they had seen a young boy standing in the dining room that ran into the darkness away from the bedroom toward the kitchen when called. Upon checking their beds, it was found that both boys were fast asleep. Needless to say, it was hard to find people to watch the boys that would stay long enough for us to leave for any length of time. Word travels fast in a small town. When our oldest son was about four years old, he would see the little boy in the corner of the upstairs bedroom. He would run by him with his eyes closed.

The man, on the other hand only appeared to our youngest and only a few times in the middle of the night. On those few occasions, I was awakened by the sound of my son screaming for someone to stop touching him and to leave him alone. Upon getting down to their room, I found that there was no one around and his brother would be fast asleep. The youngest would then point to a spot in the room and say it was a man who kept patting his head and shoulder while he tried to sleep. Obviously, we saw nothing and were completely uneasy about the whole experience. Luckily for us it only happened a few times in a month or two before it ended abruptly.

It was Fall and I had been cutting herbs and drying them in the house along with canning and freezing vegetables from the garden when all this started with the man appearing at night. I had become quite concerned and ventured out to see a woman in town who was a medium, thinking she might be able to help me figure out how to make it stop. She asked if we had been remodeling or if there were any big changes in the house that might have stirred things up. I couldn't think of anything. At the time, all I was doing was putting up the harvest from the year and working diligently on getting ready for winter. Upon explaining this to her, she asked what herbs I was drying in the house and I listed all the regulars like basil, oregano, thyme and sage. She quickly stopped me at sage and asked me to please remove it from the home and see if that helped. She thought perhaps the spirit of the man may be offended by the sage as it is used to cleanse away unwanted energy, including spirits. Just to be sure, I packed up all the herbs and even thought about taking the salt and pepper to be safe!

That night before retiring for bed, after checking on the boys, as I walked up the stairway I expressed out loud that we never intended on making anyone leave the house and that I removed the sage and there was to be no more touching EVER! I laughed to myself at the fact I had given in and talked to a ghost, but I also wasn't taking any chances. It had made all of us a bit uneasy.

Early in the morning I awoke to the eldest child standing silently at the side of the bed watching me. Startled, I awoke and asked him why he was being so creepy. He asked why the chairs were on top of the dining room table making it impossible for him and his brother to have breakfast? Still tired, I made my way downstairs, following him to the table. I could not believe my eyes as I saw all the chairs tipped upside down and piled on top of each other randomly atop the table. That was the last paranormal experience we had in the house on Prospect St. Thankfully.

There were a few stories that proceeding us buying the home. At the base of the back porch was a stone that was said to be what was left of a gravestone that one of the owners put there after it made its way through the yard acting as home plate for the neighbor kids playing baseball. Eventually, over the years, the whereabouts of the original gravesite was lost so it became a stepping stone. It was also rumored that perhaps a child was buried in the basement, but that has never been confirmed. I do know that after a year or so of silence from our paranormal housemates, there was a resurgence of activity once we moved and before it was sold. Some construction was being done to the home and I stopped by one day to check in and see how the progress was. The two men working on the house had been given a key so they could use the electric and the restroom.

Upon stopping they informed me that the house was quite noisy and they had assumed we had a dog inside or something because they heard movement for most of the day only to discover from me that the house was indeed empty. I informed them of the story concerning the paranormal and they were in disbelief.

At one time during our ownership of the home we had an investigation done which produced a recording of a little boy saying the word "no" when being asked if anyone wanted to make contact.

The knob on the door to the basement would also twist and turn and then the door itself would shake on several occasions and this had even been witnessed by guests to various get-togethers we had during our stay. My father even went so far as to sit up one night waiting for the door to rattle and then opening it time and time again to find nothing.

It was certainly a strange house and equally, an odd experience for our family, but we became accustomed to dealing with the day to day paranormal activity on a regular basis. All is much quieter these days and it is just a distant memory.

The Legend of Dogman

It is a common legend throughout Michigan that a creature comprised of part dog and part man roams the woods at night and has been seen by some and vastly scoffed at by others. Still, there is even an account of the elusive Dogman right here in Marshall and it surrounds St. Mary's Catholic Cemetery on the east end of the city. After prying into the legend further, it appears to be linked directly to the Catholic Church () here in Michigan and the story is one of love and loss.

When the Sisters of Mercy originally came to Detroit they harbored with them a secret that now has now morphed and embedded itself deep into local lore. The Sisters carried with them on the ship across the ocean from France, the Loup Garou, otherwise known as a werewolf. The werewolf, being man by day and monster by night, fell in love with one of the sisters and, while their romance was a secret, they eventually were caught when the young woman became pregnant with his child. The

Sisters and the Catholic Church banished them both and they fled Detroit into the deep oods of the Michigan forests to live forever in hiding.

Their prodigy was what we know today as Dogman. Doomed to lead a life of duality in that he looks like a dog, but walks upright like a man; he is cursed with immortality, as are his prodigy who remain hidden amongst the vast dense woods of Southern Michigan.

Somehow or another, the sightings became apparent in Marshall around Centennial Road and 18 1/2 mile. Dogman, being of Catholic descent, took refuge within the walls of St. Mary's Cemetery. It wasn't long before the church was instructed to keep him out and thus built a barbed wire fence around the perimeter. They have been unsuccessful. Many sightings have been reported within the cemetery as well as the woods surrounding the area. It is believed that secretly the caretaker, a staunch fellow at best, allows Dogman to rest in the cemetery at night regardless of his instruction and releases him in the morning before anyone can bear witness. Perhaps he feels bad or maybe he has other motives unknown, but the caretaker even keeps other animals off the property, including our horses which were asked to never return. Indeed, there is a story that had been successfully kept until now, shrouded in mystery surrounding Dogman.

Conclusion

I have said all that I wanted to say, or at least all that I could for the time being. These stories are but a breath of my life and I am forever grateful to whatever fate or wind that blew me here into little old Marshalltown. Some of these stories originated long before my time while others likely manifested during my tenure as resident ghost tour guide. It has blended together, such as truth and stories oft times do. Such as the old saying "there are no truths, only stories."

It has been quite a journey, but there are other towns now that are tucked away in the shadows of the human view that need me to uncover their stories so their characters can also gain immortality. For it would not be fair of me to favor only one and it is with fondness that I am to say goodbye to Marshall very soon.

I have been born a child here whose time was realized and is now over like the pages in this book. I had my moments and whatever it may have been, I am now freed to pursue other corners of the world that have stories to tell, other legends that lurk within local spinnings of tales.

The days of Marshall were vast and full of adventure, rich in lore and murmurs among the streets, which is what kept me longer than it should have and much shorter than planned. I'm not sure what I had hoped for in my meddling in the affairs of the locals, but it seemed almost sad if a book wasn't written. Some embraced me while others did not and it was a fine line that I walked within a city that has done its best to be sectioned off from the rest of world, only lucky enough to be found by the few. It is a great untouched secret and I was fortunate enough to be carried here by whatever breeze sought to do so. In closing, I would like to be clear that these stories are exactly as they have been told to me. Some by multiple sources and others are perhaps to the contrary. I took a best account and tried to examine all parts of each.

I believe Marshall to be one of the most haunted towns in Michigan, if not America and I would urge you to visit and dig up some old bones for yourself. At the very least, you will have stumbled into a very special place unlike anywhere in the world and perhaps find something more than you ever thought ... as I did. Just don't forget to tell them who sent you...

The End

About the Author

Brian Mason has found stories in his life, loads of stories. Stories that are odd and some that are even stranger than fiction. Stories that some would never even comprehend but they are all inside of him, ingrained in his very being, given to him as a gift. They make up his total composition and they are the fabric of his world both fictional and real. Along with stories come the people who tell them. They are characters enough for a book of their own.

From his earlier years, born and raised in Port Sanilac, Michigan to his current city of Marshall, Brian has taken great care in cultivating stories of the people he has met. His inspiration comes from the many characters and places he has known and experienced in his life. He has always maintained that most people wouldn't even believe him even if they heard his life story from his own lips, that he has lived a life of magical inspiration from his birth. The characters of his youth living in a small lakeside town, cultivated in Brian a deep passion and the drive and ability to see into the depths of life. He holds those people very dear to his heart. He is a true teller of tales and a mystery in and of himself, complex with a veil of simplicity. *Haunted Marshall* is his first paranormal collection but certainly not his last as he is currently on to the next adventure, the next story awaiting him. It has taken years of life to finally be able to sit down and share them with you.

Brian currently lives in Marshall, MI with his wife Courtney and their three children. He enjoys singing, storytelling, gardening and his furry kids. When his family is not in Marshall, they are likely at their favorite place, Sanibel Island, where they enjoy shelling and the ocean breeze.

He has been an entrepreneur, professional musician and writer for many years and has traveled extensively on and off throughout his life. He has been known by many, in more recent years, as the "ghost man" or "carriage man" of Marshall collecting stories and legends while operating his famous Marshall Carriage Co. & Ghost Tours. He has spent the past nine years collecting tales for this book.

Marshall, Michigan, the almost town, or little town that

couldn't, rests in the heart of the state. It was founded in 1839-ish, depending on which sign you read and has had a vast history of successes and failures, including losing the vote for State Capitol. From the gun-slinging saloon days to the cocaine rush, some claim Marshall is defined by her houses but I maintain she is defined by the lingering secrets that roam those pale dusty hallowed halls who have awaited their story told, who awaited my arrival.

I have claimed Marshall to be the most haunted town in Michigan and that lies mainly on the fact that in all my travels I have yet to encounter a town with such a vast collection of paranormal experiences that have either been passed down or made up, perhaps even by me. It is, in part, a game of telephone, but deeply rooted in every story is the spark from which it had its inception, a truth. It is said that there are no truths but only stories and perhaps that fact remains, yet it is in the story that we find the imagination of the very people by whom they were constructed.

This is a book for anyone's collection. It is a living history and a map for your own tour of the mysterious town of Marshall. By chance you have found it and with gratefulness I am able to share it with you.

Hauntingly,
Brian Mason